M000032774

I Love You More Than Tongue Can Tell

A Whole Mess of Poems and Songs

By: Sean-Riley Cunningham

Independently Published by Sean-Riley Cunningham
Copyright © 2022 Sean-Riley Cunningham
All Rights Reserved
ISBN 978-1-7923-9356-3
Book Designed by Ellen Gasper

"I love you more than tongue can tell!"

-My Maw

Thank you,

Bryan, David, Ethan, Maw and Paw, Patrick,
Madeleine and Lily, Jesse, Maddie Grace, Robbie Hagan,
WG, Brad, Dr. Crawford, Mrs. D'Eramo, and Ellen

I love you all.

Table of Contents

Poems

Songs

Poems

(For Readin')

The Poet and The Player

A proud proprietor of a hut clinging to the west Irish hills,
The Player, miscast as shepard, grazed and led his sheep
His dreams were to his profession as grain to a mill
Yet a belly-length beard laid his ambition into a wistful sleep
The hills recall his speeches as keenly as the warbler's cheep
Until his passion suddenly stirred at the arrival of a letter
His several possessions flung in a heap
Skipping and whistling to port, dawning his only sweater

The Player sailed to see him
A strapping French lad, mulling in a vineyard, as he ought
Planted in the island of Corsica, tucked against the sea's brim
The Poet toiled in the fields, though his labor can't be bought
His work was exchanged to better the French he'd been taught
He wrote by candle at night
Mostly of love; whether he knows it or not
Five summers escaped him, as he suspected they might

The Player hit land as his ears caught a laugh they were fond of
He is welcomed with wine and a wealth only they could spend-
The only currency worth greater than love;
The humor of a friend.
They wrote plays dawn to dusk, burning the candle at each end
Demanding its performance "au Le Musée Du Louvre !"
Boasting to the warm fields lacking ears to lend
"C'est incroyable ! C'est formidable ! Un chef-d'œuvre !"

Of course such a reunion only time could betray
The Player regretfully had to be on his way
They clutched together, more grateful than tongue could say
For the gift of words to write, and parts to play

To the Beach!

One can't help but think that maybe all
Regardless of self-inflicted circumstance
Deserve to ponder that gaudy scrawl
Our sun makes as it teeters and trundles toward tomorrow

Famished

You fling a glance my way
I catch and carefully covet it
Tuck it tenderly 'twixt my thoughts
My heart and mind scrape and scratch
Ripping and gnawing at one another
Like starved hounds, over scrap

Owie

The wound on my chest has finally healed

I peeled the skin of my breast back layer by layer
My ribs have been dissolved into nothing
My muscles atrophied from disuse
I have cracked open my heart
And placed you directly inside
To ease the pang and discomfort
And I've grown more tender with each passing day
A thing I have always feared
To surrender my offenses, salt the earth sparingly,
And lay prostrate in the hands of handsome deceit
Unflinchingly apathetic of temptation
Take the multitudes of me again and again
Introduce to me reconciliation
I will drain myself of conceit for love
I have melted my impurities into molten
This pride has been left
With my things on your nightstand
The proof that I will never need again
That the skin and tendons and muscle
That were surrendered from me
Were another man's
And that he must need them more than I

The wound on my chest has finally healed

The Shepherd

The Shepherd is blinded by no transgressions.
A Shepherd's primary responsibility,
Is the safety and welfare of the flock.
A Shepherd will graze the flock,
Lead them to areas of good forage,
And wait till the sun sets.

He has no plans.
Nor does he look forward or backward.
He worships the gods.
He is faithful.
He is knowledgeable.
He is practical.
His path is laid before him.
Why would he deviate?

He does not speculate or imagine.
He does not pretend.
For he sees no reason to.
He does not extemporize or write.
He seeks no vibrant colors.
No foreign tastes.

He loves.
He does not question why.
He is sensible.
He is pragmatic.
He does not fear death.

His father's flesh will compost into his own
When they are plotted in the same grave.

He will see the winters.
He will see the flock.
He will see the stars.
He will see the fox.
He will see the life of The Shepherd.
No more.
He will be thankful.

His gaze will not drift into curiosity.
For if his eyes were to wander past the herd,
He loses all that retains his nature.

He was a Shepherd.
He is a Shepherd.
He will be a Shepherd.

An Old Jubilee

Years ago they learned to teach their friends
Sweet sounds from bugles blow in the streets just up above
Composers conceived, writing all odds and ends
Cities were hand in hand cross the land with the sound of love

The sound was loud and we were too
The towns were filled dancing to the tune
Harmonies and melodies they sang out to the moon
Yet I always knew the tunes were me and you

She said:

Hold on there lad
Let me tell you a thing or two
My last made me real sad
And soon so will you

Fox Hole / Mr. Rabbit

When Mr. Rabbit hops by
Just to say hi
The garden must know
He's such a swell guy

But I can't see
From down in the ground
From the fox hole you see
No one's around

In the fox hole
I breathe much slower
No company around
No comers or goers

I forget how young we were
Growing togethers a blur
In your water floated duck and turtle
Your land so fertile

I catch a plane fly overhead
Though I must be mistaken
From what I have read
In the fox hole, no chances are taken

Running with Ants

Ants crawling three or four at a time
Acorn a tree holding to climb
Flutter down the street
Waiting to see
One who flutters down the street
For me

Great grate grandpa falling ahead
Whisps of a flower clutching my bed
Crescendo plays the band
Sweat dancing down the back
They throw a brick
All the way to the very back
Man you blew it slick

Thanks

Thank you so much
For not listening
For the disinterest
For the scorn

I have buried myself in foolish company
I understand now
And I couldn't be happier
Or more bitter

Eyebrows

If you had no eyebrows
That'd be okay with me
I'd hold your head in my hands
And kiss where your eyebrows used to be

To Be Aboard

The rope passing through our hands began to burn. The skin
was torn. The wool in our sweater was soaked with blood. We
grabbed the rope and it took us up. The ship was tired as were
we. We were wet. Our lives were tied in a knot with no
untanglement. The past was dead when onboard. Smoke and
slop. Cards. Fire. Silence. All precious commodities to us now.
Rope began to burn all our hands. We had no reason. No. No
memories. They were taken by the wet. No days. Nights now.
Lights were of our lives before, and were forbidden. We would
fight for fire. We would bleed for it. We would fight for the
slop. For the new, for the quick, for the day, for the pleasure.
But we had been defeated. We were wet. To be aboard is to be
known. Truly to be known must be the consequence of our
pasts.

I Confess

Our relation to the damned passing time nears dramatic.

For when I profess:

"I am with you! You patch of pumpkins in Autumn, some burst of life, of color!"

Symbols crash, wind rushes to make its date, the poles dance doubletime, ivies bury their married columns, and the tune of all that presents itself to me falls recognizably beyond its beat.

It sweetens the milk of my disposition quick enough only for one to dream that this whirlwind of expression might have always existed, and that only through you might one release their grip on the time slithering through their hands.

However a cruel opposition awaits with a dichotomy so pained it nears irony.

For when I profess:

"You are away! Soon will we color every inch of the bland night sky! Oh yes the stars as well, every one a new hue that we birth without consideration! Soon!"

Sons and fathers become dynasties, each daisy forever a bud, the hours yawn, seconds linger, minutes loiter, and each moment stretches in the light, as a tabby cat yawning in the window, reaching out to the last click of the clock.

This dreary pace chains the heart to the notion that perhaps the rate at which the strawberries bloom in their brambles is fixed, that not a single soul may tamper with the tempo of the gentle wind, frolic or dash, that each dusk follows the path of her sisters.

I, a fool of sorts, will object to such a silly idea.

For I confess:

"The sordid days that lay draped in boundless distance are deemed unworthy of my regard, because I, after an infinite toil with wicked time in which each of its moments bare fangs to strike at my years, will stamp out the head of it under my sandal. Bending time to my own will, the first of man to so, to adjust this seemingly bemused cycle. That all our uncouplings may be incessantly fleeting, and that our glances spring eternal."

Buried by the Moon

I have been buried in uncertainty
Eroded by decisions
I have not the courage to comprehend
Even the moonlight hurts now
She suffocates me
The weight of her apathy breaks my fever
And once again I am awoken by fear
I feed from the sun and rush to judgment
Unaware of my fleeting zest
And as the earth creeps past my ankles
I wonder
Why now? What haven't I done?
And I am ground up again and again

Gillyflower and Blackberry

And she rivals the tart juice of a blackberry
The horizon's tallest tower
The fragrance of rosemary
And the hue of gillyflower

You Knew

It's okay.
I don't hate you.
Please, please know that.
You can leave.
You wonder if,
Maybe you made a mistake?
I do not wonder.
I didn't.
It's okay. It's okay.

You will affirm for me,
That there isn't much left for me to learn.
And I refuse to stay while you slowly erode from under me.

But my friend, this will be different.

I can't help but seize when you're away.
My chest caves.
My arms lurch to find nothing.
My eyes fall on your empty place.
I hear your voice.
See your pictures.
It's painful.
But the knowledge,
That I will see you again...

I would tear open my rib cage.
Fall apart.
Piece by piece.
If I knew you wouldn't return.

How Can You Sleep, On A Night Like This?

Late at night
When they quiver remembering themselves
She can't invert her contemplation
But rather she lays in fire
How sad
Correcting vocabulary of her gatekeepers
Any attempt at agitation will do tonight
To deafen the introspection
What else can a young woman do?

Peacock Feathers

Gunna submit a request
For some forehead kisses
To let the boss lady know
I'm missin' my missus

See Ya!

I do not wish to be part of the future.
I do not wish to preserve my intentions.
I do not wish to be remembered by many.

Forgotten.

Yes.

Forgotten by all might be okay for me.
I will leave a small record of my time.
And I certainly will not foolishly waste it
In an attempt to outlive myself
When I,
Frankly,
Have more important things to do.

The Circumstance of Me

I have fallen from the heights of deprecation for you
From lightning and purple rain,
From scorched earth and withered reality
Down to low and base love
The sod is wet and rich here
The trees older than my memory
Soon I will forget the chill of winters,
My skin will rise only at the command of your breathe
And never to the abrasive wind
Ignorant of the creation of this place,
I think humbly through you
I will begin to question the code I bind so firmly to
I simply can't help but to imagine
That every berry has bloomed for you
The birds rehearsed their summer songs for your arrival
That my concepts and language and disposition
Have eroded to happenstance
And that they are wildly secondary to you.

You are the circumstance of me.

Better Day

When your social matters are obtuse
Your ignorance is an apology young man
Not an excuse
You don't know and that's okay
But you will know come a better day

Even through your silly stats and charts
Love is what builds our homes
Don't forget love in the moving parts
Young man there's something bigger at play
I promise you'll know come a better day

A Standstill

When indifference coated my heart.
You think that was the start?

Yes, when I lived on the hill.
That's where you seemed to have lost your will?

I'm not sure.
It's okay, you don't have to know anymore.

Can I tell you the worst?
Always best to tackle it first.

After the hill, I contracted the fury of not being able to care.
Well, what did you do there?

I used to hate more passionately than ever before.
But you don't anymore?

Not a bit. It's difficult to try and tell.
If you do that's good. If not, that's fine as well.

It's impossible to express.
I'm sure we can take a guess.

I haven't the energy, even to hate.
It's often normal to stall or to stagnate.

My bedroom reeks of food left to rot.
The seemingly simple can become a lot.

At the drop of a hat I begin to cry.
Do you happen to know why?

I know, or rather, I believe I knew.
When you feel this way, what do you do?

Let it envelop me, let my vision go red.
Have you tried our exercises perhaps instead?

I rip out my teeth and clasp my ears.
I understand it's comfortable to hide from your fears.

My skin melts as I sink into the soil.
A waste of life, a young man left out to spoil.

Life leaks from my mouth, dripping down my chin.
What do you do in that state that you're in?

I dispel into a murky pool of acid and brine.
You're allowed to feel that pain, that's fine.

I am burning my life away due to a single thought.
However hard, it can be fought.

It clings as a lover, without twitch or convulsion.
What does it say, this notion?

"He himself might his quietus make-"
An idea pale thought alone can break.

"-with a bare bodkin".
How do you feel after they begin?

I am no longer sad.
To rid your life of such is to never be glad.

Exactly, I will never again be forced to feel.
Sounds like a pretty shitty deal.

To rid myself of desire? To exterminate pain?
That is; to die. To never inhale the sun again.

Wait-
A drastic measure and a permanent fate.

I don't want to die.
Good, neither do I.

But I've lived enough.
I know it's been rough.

To know this robe of life wasn't tailored for me.
Can you name a place you'd rather be?

Yes- I'd rather be a miner deep in the earth.
That, perhaps, may give your life worth?

Not a soul to know. Ticking meticulously in the dark.
You'd like to be forgotten, to leave no mark.

Yes, I'd emerge only to sleep, in colorless ash.
You must be careful about a whim so brash.

However, submerged and alone-
You remain a man, flesh and bone.

I dig up my desire.
You get back your fire.

And in its plot lay my plaguing indifference to rest.
An infinitely noble quest.

Filling my cave with a range of emotive bleats.
You unearth it all; the sours and sweets.

Yes. I- just want to care.
Hey. We can get you there.

-

Would you like to continue hating?
Yes, I believe I will.

It might get more difficult, it may be frustrating.
And I will trudge directly uphill.

I'm always proud of you for communicating.
Thank you for dragging me out of a standstill.

Life is Good

Life is good
Life is just
Says the polish to the rust
Life is sweet
Life's dessert
Says the gold to the dirt
Life is hard
Life is tough
Says the soft to the rough

It's all fair
And if we're kind perhaps
We'll sell you back your air
While you choke on your bootstraps

Life is fair
Life is pure
Says Venice to the Moore
Life is happy
Life is calm
Says the general to the mom
Life is pleasure
Life is numb
Says the winter to the bum

Sweet Pea Sweet Pea

Sweet pea
Sweet pea
Honey bee
Marry me
My two left feet
Will never miss a beat
Ya see?

Sweet Pea
Sweet Pea
Cherry tree
Take the key
To my full heart
We'll never be apart
Ya see?

Sweet Pea
Sweet Pea
Iced tea
We can be
Lighter than air
Gee golly what a pair
Ya see?

Martial Music

Pick up your pitchforks
Put down the plow
They ain't paid
For the sweat in our brow

Now Imma young man
And young men may be brash
But old men load the musket
And turn men like us to ash

Can't you see fellas?
Your red men don't care about you
We the people look around
Those red men beat you black and blue

The Pauper

The Pauper begins to shutter as the embedded jewels flutter under his grasp. The weight of the crown sits comfortably in his hand. He stands erect, and his ears twitch like a hound's. He silently finds he has known heavier weight than this. Time assists in the notion that perhaps there are heavier weights to be addressed. Perhaps those without jewels and gold. However, the royalty is so seductive! The dukes and nobles squabble over semantics. They are so well intentioned, he comes to find. Those that belch they aren't worthy, are correct. He knows this. The crown gleams regardless. As if no great distance could be bound to bring one closer. It would remain on the horizon, retiring with the day. Perhaps The Pauper will retire as such.

My First Flight

I didn't look up once while we were in the air
I couldn't help but gawk at all those houses
There really are so many people out there

I wish I could work every job, meet each person, each tree
That I could go down and peer inside each building
And see how my life would be

We could live every life there is to live
We would laugh with each and every little patch of people
Eat every food, speak every language, take less than we give

But, on my flight I knew
I'm okay seeing what little bit of this world
That I will in my short life, as long as it's with you

Street Sweeper

The Street Sweeper controls the night and day
Today's date grows only when that tank blasts
The last of yesterday from today's pavement
No driver or soul to conduct the salt or soap
It functions, like a blade in a saw
Regardless of those whose flesh could be cut
The people, in turn, pay the sweep no mind
They scurry and bustle and trot and scamper
To expel only enough energy in courtesy
As not to be crushed

If I were gone
Blasted down to dust
The Street Sweeper wouldn't mind
I'd be whisked away in a huff
Not a single ear would perch
Nor a single bugle blow
But surely
I'd never get off that easy
Without getting a ticket

The Bottom of Our Hearth

In our home
Down every hall
The studs now groan
From wall to wall
The floorboards creak
The mouses squeak
The porch holds the hut in a hug
Clutter fills the gutter
And when the doorbell starts to stutter
The windows will shutter
At the thought of a fresh coat of paint

Oh the roof?
Every shingle seems to gossip and mingle
They know the changing of the seasons
How it brings the windows pain
As they're pelted with dust, rust, and rain
The same rain that leaves our soil tilled and spade
Every daily day of the decade

Inside the walls
Begs a different story
Knicks and scrapes
Guts and glory
Who's to say
Whose scratch is whose?
Or what exactly
Left this and that bruise?
Well the floor and door don't keep score anymore
After all, cutting a rug is what the floor is for

Please don't forget Mr. Mailbox,
Rusted and bent
Who holds the address burned in my heart
Like a paw print in cement
Or Mrs. Rocking chair, so dramatic
Nor the lawnmower or garage
The window to the attic
Cherish every gear that can grind
Every dusty bunny you find
An entire village with its own life
All for just a few children and a wife

Please know they are your friends
They've seen your first days
Your bitter ends
Even our generous pine
Was once a stick
Now coarse as the callous
Of the man with the brick
You cannot imagine the memory
In every staple, nail, and screw
The tales they tell
Are quite a few

If you leave
If you don't come back
If you find a new wall
A great big one with a crack
How special would that be
I'd love to visit
I'll help to fix it
Maybe even for free
And when you're gone

I hope you'll know
That you are loved
From the bottom of our hearth
You are loved

Mudbug and The Poboys

Lily lily pad
Spice for ya meat
Sailed from Trinidad
Lily lily lily pad
Sweet mesquite
Lathered on by ya Grandad

The Ballet

The Passionless occurrences
Light fades from falling faces
Prowess pours asses in auditoriums
An expert oracle instructed its importance
The air tastes of feathered gold
Blue cars surround the paramount sound
Family ties choke necks in need of break
The curtain draws and the idols so bestowed with importance
are then street vendors
Why do they drink?
Establishment of rapport
Why do they attend?
As they were steered
Naves slave as sand accumulates
Change is tossed
Change is denied
Intermission
They piss
Full pockets sink heavy in the upholstery
Several couldn't endure any longer
No questions are born of any importance
Cattle trods on and on
The disciples on display crave the oracle
They are oblivious to her irrelevancy
They conclude with languid congratulation
Exuberance exits and finds its way to the blue cars
The vendors return to squalor
Coitus.
The expected.
The passionless occurrences.

Fall

I only have a handful of Falls left
I want them with you
You're all I have to remember
And nothing I want to forget

Orange

It irks us to know we will never taste your jubilance
Orange
A hue containing an entire index of matters
Those of which we are well aware
Despite our curiosity, we must not indulge in such a color
Yellow has not failed us, we believe

Yet
The Orange, in god's truth, does entice us
We've seen the interpersonal adulteration it has done
Engrossing us is an inappropriate fascination
Well aware of the havoc; the destruction
That is the catch all, friends

The Orange will strike as a flash flood
Coating The Yellow til it is Yellow no more
And as quickly as it strikes, it shall fade
Leaving colorlessness
Casting The Yellow in the role of a memory

The Busker

Trodding up ninth avenue while coated in February
Fresh off work, grime, sawdust, hobbling, like a mangy hound
Knife in tow, reading the lines of the street, reticent, wary
Scraping upstream, aching, dragging myself homebound
Blocks away, I hear him, sprouting, a weed in the ground
I recognize it, no, I couldn't, incorrect, mistaken, wrong
However ill-fit, inappropriate, I know the sound
Your favorite song

The Busker plays, a weezing speaker and an oily fretboard
A flailing ham, parody, a comedy to a man about his wit
He screeches, to disguise he's plucked the wrong chord
Notes fall by the wayside, out of tune, tone unfit
Yet, however off pitch and out of key, however churlish the skit
He plays it correct
Because it is your song, I'll admit
He plays it perfect

He seizes my attention, unmoving, screeched to a halt
Puzzled, we lock eyes, how could he know?
The Busker? Camping in the crowd, sleeping with the asphalt
Your favorite song, he's it incorporated into his road show
The neon night becomes auditorium anticipating a crescendo
A tear joins me, then it's twin, then one after the other
Approaching the end, the frog in my throat begins to grow
He concludes our melody, the favorite tune of my little brother

The Busker gifted me your song, nestled, like a deer in a glen
While you were away, only with me, through paper and pen
Having nothing comparable to offer, in his case, I toss a ten
Wanting nothing more, than to hear it again

Should I Alert The Lovers?

Should I alert the lovers?
The poets and the painters?
The sculptors of great romance?
I've studied their sonnets and songs
They told of fervor in their glances and gifts
But they couldn't have known
The warmth of your breathe
Or the fire in your stare
If they only knew
How sweeter the earth would be
How it would open up to embrace them
How tall they would grow
But I think,
Perhaps,
I might keep it for myself

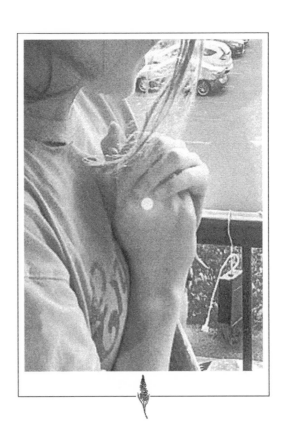

Hardly

I ain't hardly spoke
Not a single word
Bout' nothing but being blue

I ain't hardly sung no songs
That ain't about you
And the double negatives
You put me through

But I ain't hardly loved nobody
No, not nobody
Like you

Pumpkin,

I care for you still
Though your interest may tire
I promised you a life's worth of love
And I ain't no liar

Every Tree in Jersey

At seven the sun yawns and catapults herself off from the
Hudson just to kiss the tops of all the trees in Jersey. In October
they blush and anxiously shake. As she begins her morning
routine, the bus trudges on, shaking and whining, miserably so.
He has worked all night; all last night and the night before. He
is kurt and heavy but kind just the same. They seem to work in
tandem with one another. The bus and the sun. Both rise each
morning. Both help me see every tree in Jersey.

Painter? I Hardly Know Her!

Drawing a portrait of you
Is the hardest thing to do
With every stroke a serious bloke
Can't find the shade of blue

We Will Laugh

They will think of us
In another time
No, no, no
Not our names
Or traditions
But each linger in laughter
And pause between lines
If only to forgot them
To enjoy the view of another
We will be there
And we will laugh

They'll see our pictures
Our old furniture and cheap clothing
But they will notice
Our clutching together as tight as possible
And they'll feel our warmth
Our fervor
Our struggles
Our exceptional will to live beyond ourselves
And we will laugh
And we will laugh
And we will laugh

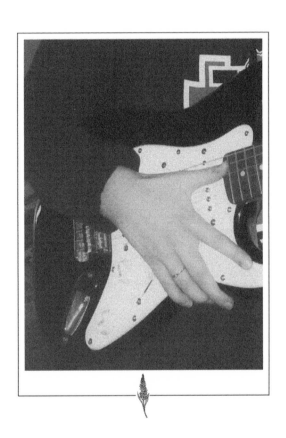

SONGS

*(F*or Singin')

Helping Hand

Peel the dead skin back but the new one won't grow
Not mighty convenient for your closing show
Build the homes of your friends and family
Better not see a single tear Mr. Manly

Please lend a helping hand
Mr. Manly Man
A helping hand
Please lend a helping hand
Mr. Manly Man
A helping hand
Please lend a helping hand

Recently it feels as though you won't learn
Confusing when I know it's what makes your heart burn
A rugged place you don't want to return
Hammers, nails, and a father's concern

The builder of the hearth
The lover since birth
Help us understand

Please lend a helping hand
Mr. Manly Man
A helping hand
Please lend a helping hand
Mr. Manly Man
A helping hand
Please lend a helping hand

The builder of the hearth

The lover since birth
Help us understand

Please lend a helping hand
Mr. Manly Man
A helping hand
Please lend a helping hand
Mr. Manly Man
A helping hand
Please lend a helping hand

Date Number One

Staring at your leg tattoo
It's almost like I know you
Look around
Take it in
Hear the sound
Of the violin
Sunshine and candlelight
Peace in their own right

Looking at the place I'm in
Let it soak into my skin
Sitting there
Writing songs
What a pair
Paper and pencil
Incomprehensible

Unknown people Unknown spaces
Made familiar at all too fast paces

Find me where they dropped me off
Where the hearts break and the light is soft

Cut my hair
Let it fall to the floor
The people around here
Are more than I can endure

The tree is chopped
It's become the dirt
The houses on top

Are more than their worth

Unknown people Unknown spaces
Made familiar at all too fast paces

Find me where they dropped me off
Where the hearts break and the light is soft

Tell me where I'm going wrong
Let's have no name for this song
Help me learn the chords
Play em' loud
Play em' proud
On my hand-me-down keyboard

The Crows Nest

The bow touches down on a western town
She picks dust and bones from the lost and found
Woman of just twenty, head fit for the crown
Suitors came and suitors went
Countless winters and summers spent
Playing lovers games and forgetting names
She wonders when her time begins
When she isn't plagued by the poet's sins
A grand return to the sea
In the crows nest, she can truly be
Of course this time has since gone by
The source of the young queen's cry
When will she find the apple, lost in her eye
By candlelight she paints her walls
Ignoring the wail of the bedrooms calls
In the midst of her reign, her health begins to faine
Her majesty withered away without a care
The desert throne would have no heir
She's found her way back to the sea
Her heart's been opened, she can truly be

Sweet Dreams Sweet Woman

Sweet Dreams Sweet Woman
A ruby in pride
An emerald in eye
I don't know how to hold you
I can't live on your land
Sweet Dreams Sweet Woman
Your love is second hand

Sweet Dreams Sweet Woman
With brushstrokes wide
Eyes bone dry
Fingers in your hair
Tell me what they said
Sweet Dreams Sweet Woman
Help me break the bread

Sweet Dreams Sweet Woman
Demeanor on fire
Soul shut tight
Lay me to rest
I must sleep now
Sweet Dreams Sweet Woman
God himself would not allow

Sweet Dreams Sweet Woman
Sacred heart and heavy head
Bleed with me instead
Sweet Dreams Sweet Woman
Sweet Dreams Sweet Woman
Sweet Dreams Sweet Woman

The Place Between The Ponds

There's a breeze that lingers just between the ponds
Where all life seems to stop and then they carry on
And the toads they croak, they croak that ugly song
Between the pond it seems, life can do no wrong

The wind it whistles by your ear
As time flies past your face
The dragonfly is in no need of almighty grace
And every year it brings you here
To remember what you've lost

And every year it brings you here
To The place between the ponds

The last time I was there I surely don't remember
Maybe I'll return one day to see what I have left
The toad's song calls to me, telling me to come home

And every year it brings me here
To the place between the ponds

Ballad For The Banshee

Electric Plug
Bed Bug
Salt on a dead slug
Teeter totter
Father daughter
She leads the lambs to slaughter

Language is dead
Meaning is wed
With the loud voice
Rejoice
It's all in your head

La la la la la la do da day
Turn up the volume if you got something to say
La la la la la la here and now
Screech your speech the eyes forever will endow

Two by four
Door to door
You're yearning for
A cigarette butt
Play the horn
Feel the scorn
The students away
Feel the breeze
In the leaves
The palm trees sway

Language is dead
Meaning is wed
With the loud voice
Rejoice
It's all in your head

La la la la la la do da day

Turn up the volume if you got something to say
La la la la la la here and now
Screech your speech the eyes forever will endow

The kids are fed
God is dead
Play a song
Cook your meat
Stomp your feet
All year long

Language is dead
Meaning is wed
With the loud voice
Rejoice
It's all in your head

La la la la la la do da day
Turn up the volume if you got something to say
La la la la la la here and now
Screech your speech the eyes forever will endow

Rocking Chair To The Shelf

A shelf filled with book spines colored red
A golden vase that showed silver reflections
Glass bottles play king of the hill
A son and matching father won't fit the bill

CocaCola at a Crossroads
Welcome to our home
Broken rutter
Blinds and shutters

Broken dish sittin' pretty in a painting's place
Roses for a show rose for a show of roses
Broken sister's face made of cheap clay
Used to be important some say

CocaCola at a Crossroads
Welcome to our home
Broken rutter
Blinds and shutters

Someone had to die for all of this
Someone had to lie for all of this
Bumble bee wings flattened between the pages
Leather bound scripture sags as it ages

CocaCola at a Crossroads
Welcome to our home
Broken rutter
Blinds and shutters

Glass holds gifts from an old umbrella
Two dollar stained glass and friendship mahogany
Exactly enough room for one more monogamy

CocaCola at a Crossroads
Welcome to our home
Broken rutter
Blinds and shutters

Jordan

If I could see my mother
She'd hit me o'er the head
For not knowin' the Jordan's flowin'
But Jordan's dried and dead

If I could cross that Jordan
I'd sit on daddy's knee
But Jordan, oh Jordan
Ain't a-flowin' for me

But I know better
If they could hear my prayer
I'd cross that big bad Jordan
And meet my folks there

Big Baby

I met a lady
We had a baby
Now baby wasn't big
But baby grew like a twig

Then one night
A terrible fright
A man with a gun
I said baby run

Now my ladys gone
But I carry on
Cause I got my big baby
Reminds me of that lady

I got my big baby
Reminds me of that lady
I'll take care of my baby
Till I'm in Hades

We moved around
We settled downtown
The years were many
Big baby turned twenty

He played the guitar
The people came far
To hear that tune
The ladies would swoon

I got my big baby
Reminds me of that lady
He'll take care of me
Till I'm 103

Yes he'll take care of me
The son of my lady

In the Sun

I'll save you the sun
While you're away
I'll collect the rain
Most every day

Catch the smell of roses
Just for you
Capture the sky
The shades of blue
For me and you

I'll keep the mornings of the spring
Memorize the songs the cardinals sing
If I was sure that it would bring
You to me
That just won't be
I know you're happy
In the sun
In the sun
In the sun

I'll pack a picnic
By the pond
Braid your hair
Strawberry blonde

I'll send a letter
By a dove
Silence the thunder
From up above
For you my love

I'll keep mornings of the spring
Memorize the songs the cardinals sing
If I was sure that it would bring
You to me

That just won't be
I know you're happy
In the sun
In the sun
In the sun

In my heart
I set you free
I know you and me
How silly
Please enjoy
And please have fun
In the sun
In the sun
In the sun

Real Life

I want a new pair of skin
A complete set with a new next of kin
A friend
A friend to pretend
A lover perhaps
A brother, a lover, a mother perhaps

Can we live by the ocean
Can we have a life of ease
Can we buy a little time
Can we, can we please

A fresh blank page
Add a dash of rage
A pink pretty bunny
Or something less funny
A serious life in the space age
Is too expensive for minimum wage

I can borrow I can steal
That doesn't make it real
I can borrow I can steal
That doesn't make it real
I can borrow I can steal
That doesn't make it real

I want a couple new eyes
Emerald green that really cries
Out for them
But their not here
But then for what?
I don't know, their not real

Can we live by the ocean
Can we have a life of ease

Can we buy a little time
Can we, can we please

A fresh blank page
Add a dash of rage
A pink pretty bunny
Or something less funny
A serious life in the space age
Is too expensive for minimum wage

I can borrow I can steal
That doesn't make it real
I can borrow I can steal
That doesn't make it real
I can borrow I can steal
That doesn't make it real

Can we live by the ocean
I can borrow I can steal
Can we have a life of ease
That doesn't make it real
Can we buy a little time
I can borrow I can steal
Can we can we please
That doesn't make it real

Boogiewoogiesugardisco

You wake up
You pour a little paint in your cup
Therapy
Ivory Brush and you're free

Fill all your negative space
Experience blocks your eyes
The sad boy needs color on his face

There's a place
That no purple's pinks can replace
Where you'll be
Artistically devine you'll see
Bitch I'm me

In a place that you design
Where all your colors run free

Boogiewoogiesugardisco
Boogiewoogiesugardisco
Come to the purple place
The purple place for people's parties
Boogiewoogiesugardisco
Boogiewoogiesugardisco
Boogiewoogiesugardisco
Boogiewoogiesugardisco

Put down your pallet and free me
Hard to quit wouldn't you agree
Artist go back where you belong
Can't you see this is my story

There's a place
That no purple's pinks can replace
Where you'll be
Artistically devine you'll see
Bitch I'm me

In a place that you design
Where all your colors run free

Boogiewoogiesugardisco
Boogiewoogiesugardisco
Come to the purple place
The purple place for people's parties
Boogiewoogiesugardisco
Boogiewoogiesugardisco
Boogiewoogiesugardisco
Boogiewoogiesugardisco

Boogiewoogiesugardisco
Boogiewoogiesugardisco
Come to the purple place
The purple place for people's parties
Boogiewoogiesugardisco
Boogiewoogiesugardisco
Boogiewoogiesugardisco
Boogiewoogiesugardisco

Herky Jerky

What a strange thought to be free of thought
To rot away in a tiny box
I'm not afraid to perish
Who knows if I would cherish
These days I've spent walking
The days I've spent talking to my father
On the phone

All alone now
All alone now

Gravity hurts me
I feel herky jerky
And I miss my mom
I miss my mom

Gravity hurts me
I feel herky jerky
And I miss my mom
I miss my mom

Is this better than forgetting
More noble than regretting
I ought to fight for that feeling
But I have no choice but to rest
My bones are telling me
You did your best

As I Travel West

As I Travel West
Two flies land on my head
I know they want what's best
I ignore the things they've said

I ain't the moss on the tree
People with no faces
As far as the eye can see

I'm diggin
I'm diggin
I'm diggin
I'm diggin

For gold

As I travel west
Bulls hide from the sun
On track on their idle quest
Only God knows when their done

I ain't the moss on the tree
People with no faces
As far as the eye can see

I'm diggin
I'm diggin
I'm diggin
I'm diggin

For gold

As I travel west
Vultures circle over head
I lay down on the trail to rest

The earth is quick to make me a bed

I ain't the moss on the tree
People with no faces
As far as the eye can see

I'm diggin
I'm diggin
I'm diggin
I'm diggin

For gold

I'm diggin
I'm diggin
I'm diggin
I'm diggin

For gold

Twins

This old bed misses her twin
And this here dresser
Knows where you might've been
If I hadn't gone west
Thoughts and prayers
I send you the best

A steel cross hung above the frame of the door
Thirty square feet, no more
Beds, dressers, and things
Clothes blocked the floor
Like muddy december snow
That wouldn't stick to the ground
No matter the month you'd be around

This old bed misses her twin
And this here dresser
Knows where you might've been
If I hadn't gone west
Thoughts and prayers
I send you the best

Only a quick eye followed our conversation
Language of our own creation
Flowers, records, and things
Moons and stars stuck to the ceiling
Slowly came down year after year
No matter whether you'd be here

This old bed misses her twin
And this here dresser
Knows where you might've been
If I hadn't gone west
Thoughts and prayers
I send you the best

This old bed misses her twin
And this here dresser
Knows where you might've been

If I hadn't gone west
If I hadn't gone west
If I hadn't gone west
Thoughts and prayers
I send you the best

Helena Troy

Helena Troy had nothing to say
For two weeks I knew where my head would lay
A cool cats hands so full of rings
And thoughts so full of better things
Your family tree woven so complexly
I know your dogs and sisters will forget me

But I was happy
But I was happy
But I was happy

We gave each other just exactly what we needed
A certain kind of touch
That was selectively breeded
What the fuck is love and why can't I say it
I guess cause I don't know you and you'd probably

Skip town
Don't leave now
Settle down
Stay with me
Family
Secretly
I'd marry thee
But actually
Go away
Leave today
There's no much else that we can play

Good ole'
Helena Troy had nothing to say
For two weeks I knew what that girl would say
I looked at you for so long
There's nothing we can do to prolong
I wish you could stay but I want you to go
I can't forget your love for Van Gough

You were happy
You were happy
You were happy

I gave you color which you gave placement
I hope you keep the necklace I'll keep the bracelet

But we'll forget the date
You know it's fate
Thoughts migrate
But I loved you
Cause I loved me
And thankfully
You were you
And I hope I
Could satisfy
Your need for love
At the end of the day
There's nowhere where else for us to stay

Helena Troy had not much to say
For two weeks I knew where my head would lay
A cool cats hands so full of rings
And thoughts so full of better things
Your family tree woven so complexly
I know your dogs and sisters will forget me

Helena Troy had not much to say
For two weeks I knew where my head would lay
A cool cats hands so full of rings
And thoughts so full of better things
Your family tree woven so complexly
I know your dogs and your sisters will forget me

But I was happy

Apple's Tree

I'm starting to think momma wasn't always right
That life out of Eden isn't such a sore sight
I wish I could sing her a song of new life
Then they'd put down the pitchforks and grab a putty knife
To sculpt a new breed with a new sixth sense
They'd live in the future and love the present tense
Cities would grow, soil would be rich
No more quarrels over which man is which

Momma please tell me, What's so lovely
About the apple falling so near the tree

Once you get out you'll never come in
And with all that you learned, you'd better trust your kin
They share what they can and covet the rest
Whoever stocks the most must surely be blessed
Busts made from gold and named carved in bricks
For the cost of your soul they'll sell you their tricks
Mommas play this game too, though they'll certainly lie
The forbidden fruit makes delicious apple pie

Momma please tell me, What's so lovely
About the apple falling so near the tree

Momma please tell me, What's so lovely
About the apple falling so near the tree

Momma
Me
Momma
Tree
Momma
Me
Momma
Tree

Andromeda's Cricket Tune

On a pink night
Is where I found you
Andromeda
I was blue
Holes in my boots
From walking so far
Following the light
Of my soul star

A pink light
Shown bright
I think tonight I'll sit and write

I hear her in the cricket tune
I see her in the deep blue moon
Andromeda
I love you
I'm finally ready
We're going steady
It's true loves debut

Andromeda you're so warm
Andromeda
Andromeda you're so warm
Andromeda

Shine on me
I'll see you soon
Let me hear the cricket tune
Andromeda
I love you

I hear her in the cricket tune
I see her in the deep blue moon
Andromeda
I love you
I'm finally ready
We're going steady
It's true loves debut

Bubby's Dead

Adam and Eve went
Every hot summer spent
The garden of eden
Stampedin'
On the land lent by the lord
Good lord and now my faiths bent
Apples to apples
Dust to dust
She grapples with serpent
And the night's locus

The dogs ran wild
The child's singlefile
He tried to walk a mile
Now his brothers on trial

My bubby is all but dead
I ain't my brothers keeper
Now he's losing his head

Drivin daddy's cattle
Sittin' loose in the saddle
Hidin' my face
When the sky begins to rattle
"Sonny sonny
Ain't it funny
You're destitute
You squashed the fruit
Of your mummy"

The dogs ran wild
The child's singlefile
He tried to walk a mile
Now his brothers on trial

My bubby is all but dead

I ain't my brothers keeper
Now he's losing his head

A bright light from the night
Began to shine
A holy sign god devine
Scared away the bovine
Lying straight to the lord
Now he's walkin' a fine line
A shiver down his spine
While he frowns upon his bloodline

The dogs ran wild
The child's singlefile
He tried to walk a mile
Now his brothers on trial

My bubby is all but dead
I ain't my brothers keeper
Now he's losing his head

What's Wrong?

The mighty gods are gone
The swords have been withdrawn
Who, oh sweet mercy
Can we place blame on

The poor are sick and dead
The rich have lost their heads
Who's word, oh sweet mercy
Can we spread

How can we do any wrong
How can we do any wrong
How can we do any wrong

If we were left here all alone
To find out on our own
How far that we have grown
And who would take the throne

Would we know which man is right
How long would we fight
Who's word would we wright
Would day become night

How can we do any wrong
How can we do any wrong
How can we do any wrong
Let's see
How can we do any wrong
How can we do any wrong
How can we do any wrong

How do we know
Where do we go
How can we do any wrong
Where do we belong

How can we do any wrong
How can we do
How can we do
How can we do

Close All The Papers

How could you say that said the fancyman
The papers read that I'm a dirty crook
Don't they know it hurts my feelings
He paid his weight in gold I'm told
To bury his dirty dealings

Crush the little man
Put out his fire slowly
Just a gentle nudge
To let him know he's lowly

The writers room took shelter
From the lawyers who reigned from above
For they were to buried straight away
Because apparently it's illegal explains the paralegal
To tell the truth unless you can pay

Crush the little man
Put out his fire slowly
Just a gentle nudge
To let him know he's lowly

Years and years the battle waged while
The papers precious pockets grew thin
The lawyers trumped every paper sold
Though it doesn't matter who wins the legal chatter
The paper would of course have to fold

Crush the little man
Put out his fire slowly
Just a gentle nudge
To let him know he's lowly

Crush the little man
Put out his fire slowly
Just a gentle nudge

To let him know he's lowly

Slapp them on the back
Get them to pick up the slack

Slapp them on the back
Get them to pick up the slack

Slapp them on the back
Get them to pick up the slack

Silly Songs / True Blue

Maybe I write too biblically
Maybe I love too silly-ly
Maybe my word choice is slippery
Maybe I don't carry the weight of the earth
But I wait for the birth of a thought that's new
A true blue thought that no one ever knew
I brew and I brew and I think it through and through
But I just can't knew
A true blue thought that no one ever knew

Maybe my thoughts are for you and me
Maybe I ain't so seriously
Maybe I could work on delivery
Maybe I don't carry the weight of the earth
But I wait for the birth of a thought that's new
A true blue thought that no one ever knew
I brew and I brew and I think it through and through
But I just can't knew
A true blue thought that no one ever knew

A true blue thought that no one ever knew
I brew and I brew and I think it through and through
But I just can't knew
A true blue thought that no one ever knew

True blue
True blue
True blue
True blue
True blue
True blue

Goodbye

When you died Jade
Did it hurt
It couldn't have been worse
Than anything
You felt on earth

I thought you'd die before I did
But you
You were certain
You would make sure of it

I hope the soil slurps your skin
The moths play dress up in your clothes
I wish the longest brightest days
For your next of kin
That only I wonder
What could have been

I hope the soil slurps your skin
The moths play dress up in your clothes
I wish the longest brightest days
For your next of kin
That only I wonder
What could have been

I hope the bugs snuggle up in your bed
The lovers all recite your words
You're revered in this time
I hope now that you've gone ahead
That I am the only one
Who needs to forgive what you've said

I hope the soil slurps your skin
The moths play dress up in your clothes
I wish the longest brightest days
For your next of kin

That only I wonder
What could have been

When you died Jade
Did it hurt
It couldn't have been worse
Than anything
Than anything
Than anything
You felt on earth

You Wouldn't Believe it Annabelle

You wouldn't believe it Annabelle
The city really does never rest
I'm hoping you're well Annabelle
I'm wishing you the best

You wouldn't believe it Annabelle
The concrete has a glitter veneer
They say it's for grip in the winter season
But I just know if you were here
You'd make up a much funner reason

You wouldn't believe it Annabelle
The size of the world
With all of the time
I have all the things to do
Nothing could be better
Nothing of course
But sharing it with you

You wouldn't believe it Annabelle
When it's rains, the buildings get lost in the clouds
Maybe they're chasing the stars
We seemed to have lost them in the crowds

You wouldn't believe it Annabelle
All the languages so foreign to my ear
Calling their children and dogs
All the lovely words to the ones they hold dear

You wouldn't believe it Annabelle
The size of the world
With all of the time
I have all the things to do
Nothing could be better
Nothing of course

But sharing it with you

You wouldn't believe it Annabelle
How fast the leaves fall, fall and turn to grey
Time, he's so hasty
I'm sure you've heard him say
Annabelle I will rush when you're in love
And drag when you're away

You wouldn't believe it Annabelle
The size of the world
With all of the time
I have all the things to do
Nothing could be better
Nothing of course
But sharing it with you

Pick My Brain

Pick my brain baby
You can pick my brain
Check that grey matter maybe
Pick pick pick my brain
And if you pick my brain baby
All that you will find
Is that your always on my mind

From the very first date
She's my every thought
Every other lady
I've now forgot

She's on my brain
Shes in my head
It's driving me insane
When we're gunna be wed

Pick my brain baby
You can pick my brain
Check that grey matter maybe
Pick pick pick my brain
And if you pick my brain baby
All that you will find
Is that your always on my mind

Well I don't know
The spell I'm under
But not for a second
Did I ask or wonder

I said not a word
No not a peep
It must be love
Cause I can't sleep

Pick my brain baby
You can pick my brain
Check that grey matter maybe
Pick pick pick my brain
And if you pick my brain baby
All that you will find
Is that your always on my mind

Now with the brain
Is his friend the heart
And they never agree
Even to stop or start

But now they met you
And they both agree
Ain't nothing more right
Than you lovin me

Pick my brain baby
You can pick my brain
Check that grey matter maybe
Pick pick pick my brain
And if you pick my brain baby
All that you will find
Is that your always on my mind

Sugaree

Elizabeth gave herself that name
Cause her parents couldn't stake no claim
In a girl with a banjo in her hand

Elizabeth was music alive
Saved that three dollar seventy-five
For a year
To get a guitar in her hand

She played that thang ol upside down
That Carolina girl traveled town to town
Do da day da do da da do da dee

And she'd shake and play that sugaree
Sweeter than the music of a honey bee
Dum dum dum dum tweedledee
Shake mama play that sugaree

Elizabeth kept the guitar in her head
She mighta thought that tune was dead
Till the trip that day to the store

Elizabeth ran right back to square one
That tune then began to begun
At 60 years
The guitar felt right in her hand

She played that thang ol upside down
That Carolina girl traveled town to town
Do da day da do da da do da dee

And she'd shake and play that sugaree
Sweeter than the music of a honey bee
Dum dum dum dum tweedledee
Shake mama play that sugaree

Elizabeth, everyone knew that name
A right side up girl with all the fame
Kissed the guitar in hand

Elizabeth got to about ninety-four
Said I ain't never been this bored before
And hopped a freight train
With her guitar in her hand

She played that thang ol upside down
That Carolina girl traveled town to town
Do da day da do da da do da dee

And she'd shake and play that sugaree
Sweeter than the music of a honey bee
Dum dum dum dum tweedledee
Shake mama play that sugaree

She played that thang ol upside down
That Carolina girl traveled town to town
Do da day da do da da do da dee

And she'd shake and play that sugaree
Sweeter than the music of a honey bee
Dum dum dum dum tweedledee
Shake mama play that sugaree

Thicket of White Noise

Fire again
We missed her boys
She jumped the fence
Through the thicket
Of white noise

We'll try again tomorrow
She'll be back in the morning
And when she collects all my dreams
We will shoot without warning

She's gathered my exhaustion
She's spent it elsewhere
Shoot her dead boys
Another night I couldn't bear

When she returns
At the break of day
Please not so close
Don't let her fog
Lead you astray

We'll try again tomorrow
She'll be back in the morning
And when she collects all my dreams
We will shoot without warning

She's gathered my exhaustion
She's spent it elsewhere
Shoot her dead boys
Another night I couldn't bear

Did it hurt?

Let's talk like we did before
Let me remember without the hurt
Let's know what lied in store
Before I can't stand it any longer
You taught me all I know
I'm seeking to forget

Go away
Go away
Go away
Go away

I'm seeking to forget
Did we hurt them?
Did they cry?
When they heard the snare drum?
Do you really know why?
Did they?
When we fell from the sky?
Were our skies clearer?
Was heaven nearer?

I can't be sorry
It's out of my hands
My sorrow is woven
In foreign lands

Silly Boy

You've been ground into the earth
The sound of the hearth and
Keening of the saints
Intoxicate you now
Fields of wheat and golden imagery weren't enough for you
The endless feast of horrid beast
The gift of the fine, fun, flying, and fancy free

And the spoiled brat who ate the fat
From the silver spoon
Found the ground on the way to the womb

Silly Boy
You've tasted honey and milk
Silly Boy
Your hands are numb to the silk
Silly Boy
You had it all
It was your downfall
The taste of silver

Leaves of gold reflected the lust of the sun
Into your heavy pallet
You fought for more but how much more
Before you swore your gut was full
You speak percents that flutter in your speech that's simply
Exclusion, collusion, abrasion and hateful persuasion

And the fat cat who ate the brat
Under the full moon
Promised he'd be back before noon

Silly Boy
You've tasted honey and milk
Silly Boy
Your hands are numb to the silk

Silly Boy
You had it all
It was your downfall
The taste of silver

Christopher

Christopher
It isn't cold enough for the snow to stick
Watch the ground the ice is slick
Remember the trick pick up your feet

Christopher
Did I mention?
Christopher
Christopher
Pay Attention

Where are you
Where are you
Christopher

Where are you
Where are you
Christopher

Where are your
Where are you
Christopher

The light from the stars won't let me sleep
Christopher
The weight of the sun won't let me weep
Christopher

Christopher
It isn't cold enough for the snow to stick
Watch the ground the ice is slick
Remember the trick pick up your feet

Christopher
Did I mention?
Christopher

Christopher
Pay Attention

Where are you
Where are you
Christopher

Where are you
Where are you
Christopher

Where are your
Where are you
Christopher

The officers say it's been too long
Christopher please come home
I know your lost you don't know where to go
Your red boots still treading the virgin snow

Where are you
Where are you
Christopher

Where are you
Where are you
Christopher

Where are you
Where are you
Christopher

The light from the stars won't let me sleep
Christopher
The light from the sun won't let me weep
Christopher

Christopher

It isn't cold enough for the snow to stick
Watch the ground the ice is slick
Remember the trick pick up your feet

Christopher
Christopher
Christopher

Dear Annabelle,

Your heartbeat sounds like yellow spring
When you love hard, when you dance and sing

You fill my lungs like a handful of breeze
Sweet and strong like the honeybees
I can't wait to see you wear my clothes
To kiss your head, to tap your nose
To lay in bed, to quickly doze

I pray you sing in the wind
That you allow moss to fill your heart
And let yellow sunlight fill your eyes
Because you are a gracious flower
A rainbow after a spring shower
You are forever a vibrant soul
A record chock full of rock n' roll

I wish you honeysuckle
I wish you lemonade
I wish you songbirds
I wish you summer shade

You make me happy
You make me happy
You make me happy

Love,
Jesse

Regression

We're In regression

We're in regression
We're in regression
We're in regression
It's begun again

Can't grow in the concrete crack
Can't grow in the concrete crack
Backseat in the Cadillac on the Racetrack
Can't grow in a throwback
Can't grow in a throwback
Picture of the old shack on the Kodak

Move mortar move brick
Let's get better
Move gold move quick
I am the pacesetter

I don't know if I can contribute to an eb and flow
That goes so fast past progression
The profession of risen aggression against moving forward
The border of self-expression
The hoarder of any aggression
While Sisyphus rolled that rock we bought and sold his stock
It's all the same, but don't think for a minute
We came to pick a name to blame
They got to decide
That pride keeps us stepping in time with arms beside
We chirp and chime that we've taken two steps forth
"Don't worry brothers and sisters we're headed true north"
We beg to differ
We're on a track of which you can only turn left
A path bereft of change
Starving children bragging on their full bellies
Nagging on pacesetters with legs like jelly

But if against the current we fight
We can only turn right

Can't grow in the concrete crack
Can't grow in the concrete crack
Can't grow in the concrete crack
Can't grow in the concrete crack
Can't grow in the concrete crack
Can't grow in the concrete crack
Can't grow in the concrete crack
Can't grow in the concrete crack

My Oh My

Your comedy's too on the nose
You're trying on big sissy's clothes
Good god don't talk so loud
Good god don't be so proud

Your comedy's too on the nose
You're trying on big sissy's clothes
Good god don't talk so loud
Good god don't be so proud

Is there eternal damnation
For the dead generation
Brimstone and Fire
For those who desire
To be free
What layer of hell
For those who rebel
Those like me

My oh my
My oh my
My oh my
My oh my

Your comedy's too on the nose
You're trying on big sissy's clothes
Good god don't talk so loud
Good god don't be so proud

Your comedy's too on the nose
You're trying on big sissy's clothes
Good god don't talk so loud
Good god don't be so proud

We will play
We will dance

We will scrap
For a chance
For a seat
At the table
For a feat
To be able
To..

My oh my
My oh my
My oh my
My oh my

Your comedy's too on the nose
Your trying on big sissy's clothes
Good god don't talk so loud
Good god don't be so proud

Your comedy's too on the nose
My oh my
Your trying on big sissy's clothes
My oh my
Good god don't talk so loud
My oh my
Good god don't be so proud
My oh my

The Finger

A great mistake when I was twenty
Was breaking my back for short shit money
Ass crack of dawn on a bus to Jersey
Workin for a man who didn't care about me

Now I lost a finger in the end of November
Not a great move for a union non-member
Doc said don't worry son we'll get you on track
You'll be breaking your back by next December

Told boss man what the doctor had to say
Bout the unfortunate accident yesterday
Said he'd get down on both knees and pray
But hell would freeze over before he would pay

Now I struggle with picking six strings
Workin' with my hands
Hammers drills and things
To this day my pain still lingers
From when I gave boss man the finger

Sittin at home and shit outta luck
With a big ole cast I'm lame as a duck
Week after week of watchin' news on TV
The politicians say they really care about me

My landlord asks when I'll pay my rent
I try to tell him how outta shape I'm bent
I sold all my saws, my hammers and drills
To cover all my medical bills

Now I been playin' guitar and doin what I can
Beggin for cash in a Folgers coffee can
He said how you play with nine fingers is funny
But you're on the street if I don't get my money

Now I struggle with picking six strings
Workin' with my hands
Hammers drills and things
To this day my pain still lingers
From when I gave boss man the finger

Now I'm out and left for dead
Dreaming my dreams on a concrete bed
A passerby tapped me on the head
It was my ole boss man here's what he said

It's the middle of the day now, boy wake up
Then he tossed a nickel and a dime in my cup
Ain't you tired of livin' like a slob?
Dust yourself off and go get a job

Now I struggle with picking six strings
Workin' with my hands
Hammers drills and things
To this day my pain still lingers
From when I gave boss man the finger

Now I struggle with picking six strings
Workin' with my hands
Hammers drills and things
To this day my pain still lingers
From when I gave boss man the finger

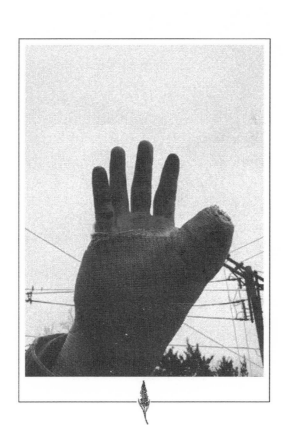

Sick Day / What to do

What to do
What to do
What to do
What to do
What to do

Heavy cough
Jerkin' off
Playing video games

Sick day
The only way
To pass the time

What to do
What to do
What to do
What to do
What to do

Who am I fooling
They know I'm alright
They know I'm drooling
Sleeping fine through the night

What to do
What to do
What to do
What to do
What to do

My pj's
My eyes glaze
I roll another joint

TV
I watch for free
I got the password

What to do
What to do
What to do
What to do
What to do

Who am I fooling
They know I'm alright
They know I'm drooling
Sleeping fine through the night

Today I'm jumping off the clock
Every single call will get a block
Oh I'm feeling fine
No fever I'll admit
Yes I was up at nine
But I today ain't doing shit

What to do
What to do
What to do
What to do
What to do

Take a nap
Feed the cat
Lay around awhile

Order food
Tip the dude
My pay for the day

What to do
What to do

What to do
What to do
What to do

Who am I fooling
They know I'm alright
They know I'm drooling
Sleeping fine through the night

Today I'm jumping off the clock
Every single call will get a block
Oh I'm feeling fine
No fever I'll admit
Yes I was up at nine
But I today ain't doing shit

Pull a Punch

If you pull just one punch
There's no race
If you pull just one punch
You're second place
If you pull just one punch
They'll have you for lunch

Why are you panting
Seems you run just to catch a breath
You've decided we're enemies
And you're fighting to the death

If you pull just one punch
There's no race
If you pull just one punch
You're second place
If you pull just one punch
They'll have you for lunch

Not writing anything
So you can't be read
Reveals a mouthful more
Than anyone's said

Five six seven eight
Five six seven eight
Five six seven eight
Five six seven eight
Five six seven eight

Why are you panting
Seems you run just to catch a breath
You've decided we're enemies
And you're fighting to the death

If you pull just one punch

There's no race
If you pull just one punch
You're second place
If you pull just one punch
They'll have you for lunch

Bubba please slow down
At this rate you'll collapse
But I know as soon as you wake
You'll relapse

Five six seven eight
Five six seven eight
Five six seven eight
Five six seven eight
Five six seven eight

Why are you panting
Seems you run just to catch a breath
You've decided we're enemies
And you're fighting to the death

If you pull just one punch
There's no race
If you pull just one punch
You're second place
If you pull just one punch
They'll have you for lunch

Bluebird

Bluebird
What have you done
You're lost my friend
In this web you've spun

We learned to fly from you
Swept up in the breeze
Hearing your tender coo
High as the honeybees
I'm drinking morning dew

Bluebird
Don't get caught
Heaven Heaven Heaven
Never seemed so blue

Old friend
Come down to earth
Your nest is full for what it's worth

You're safe in your tree
The seasons change
That's a guarantee
Love is strange
And we both agree

Bluebird
Don't get caught
Heaven Heaven Heaven
Never seemed so blue

You're drinking morning dew
I learned from you
Swaying in the breeze
High as honeybees

Bluebird
Don't get caught
Heaven Heaven Heaven
Never seemed so blue

Bluebird
I feel your pain
Put your wings away
It's about to rain

You've carried me
Through peaceful calm and tragedy
A loving psalm of our family tree

Heaven never seemed so blue

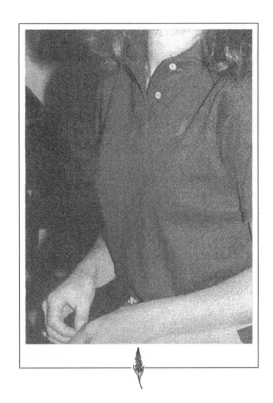

Our Place

Your pillow filled with peacock feathers
Letters from when the weather wasn't better
We're in love and we take bubble baths
The poetry doesn't stay in our drafts

The plants are yellow
And the sky says hello
And the sunflowers bellow
That you love that fellow
The window's cactus sets the mood
Tells me to kiss with a mouthful of food

When we wash our face
You give me love
You give me grace
At our place

Whispering with the walls so thin
Call your mom, tell her how we been
Paint my face with forehead kisses
An hour away and I'm missin' my missus

With your yellow pants
And the sky's flirty dance
A quick lover's glance
From the sunflower plants
Waking up to strawberry shampoo
I can't write if it ain't about you

When you hold my face
I'm a young man

In your embrace
At our place
At our place
At our place

The Protest Party

The war on poverty
Fought by ya mama's sovereignty
The wage gap won't close
If the poor can't afford spirituality
Cause

Cousins and kin
Wrasslin' over what mighta' been
Can't you see fella
Can't you see
You ain't no Rockefeller
You'll be like me
You'll be with me
In The Protest Party

Our mission is plain
Oh brothers can't you feel the strain
You ain't got nothing in common
With your fat cat lawman
Fill the streets let 'em hear the sound
Burn that Target to the fucking ground

Cousins and kin
Wrasslin' over what mighta' been
Can't you see fella
Can't you see
You ain't no Rockefeller
You'll be like me
You'll be with me
In The Protest Party

Nothing's right
Nothing's just
Investments are light
In the people's trust

Nothing's right
Nothing's just
Investments are light
In the people's trust

Nothing's right
Nothing's just
Investments are light
In the people's trust

Cousins and kin
Nothing's right

Wrasslin' over what mighta' been
Nothing's just

Can't you see fella
Investments are light

Can't you see
In the people's trust

You ain't no Rockefeller
Nothing's right

You'll be like me
Nothing's just

You'll be with me
Fire burns bright

In The Protest Party
Before it's dust

Here! I've Fallen in Love

The people you meet they all can't forget you
Their tattoos and keychains just won't allow
Recipes, hairstyles, the words that slip into your mouth
Computer passwords are proof that loves just endures

So many last names
So many picture frames
Are with you now
Not a person is truly whole
When you carry just a tad
Of those who touch your soul

Where is there but here
You can fall in love so deep and secure
In love with the middle names
The hopes and the games
The forever fleeting fervor

The people you meet you'll always recall
Their birthdays, favorite colors, and scars
Quotes, clothing, the words that slip into your mouth
Favorite songs are proof that loves just endures

So many last names
So many picture frames
Are with you now
Not a person is truly whole
When you carry just a tad
Of those who touch your soul

Where is there but here

You can fall in love so deep and secure
In love with the middle names
The hopes and the games
The forever fleeting fervor

Thank you.

Made in the USA
Monee, IL
13 November 2022

8acf2bdd-da03-4e41-b830-d79db3039236R01